I0446743

Table Of Contents

Chapter 1: Introduction to Starting a Non-Profit Organization

Understanding Non-Profit Organizations

Non-profit organizations play a vital role in society by addressing various social, environmental, and community needs. If you have a desire to make a positive impact and are considering starting a non-profit organization, it is essential to understand the basics of how these organizations operate and the process of obtaining tax-exempt status.

This subchapter aims to provide a comprehensive understanding of non-profit organizations, their purpose, structure, and the steps involved in establishing tax-exempt status. Whether you have a specific cause in mind or want to help your community in general, this guide will help you navigate the process smoothly.

To begin with, a non-profit organization is a legally recognized entity that operates for a specific purpose other than generating profit for its members or owners. Instead, the primary goal of non-profits is to serve the public interest and fulfill their mission. Understanding the purpose and mission of your non-profit is crucial, as it will guide your organization's activities and decision-making processes.

Non-profit organizations are typically structured as corporations, associations, or trusts. Each structure has its own set of advantages and requirements, so it's important to choose the one that aligns best with your organization's goals and needs. This subchapter will help you understand the differences and make an informed decision.

Once you have a clear understanding of the purpose and structure, the next step is to obtain tax-exempt status. This status enables your organization to receive tax-deductible donations and grants, making it more attractive to potential donors. The process of obtaining tax-exempt status involves filing an application with the Internal Revenue Service (IRS) and meeting specific criteria outlined in the tax code.

This subchapter will provide you with a step-by-step guide on filing for tax-exempt status. From gathering necessary documents to completing the application forms, we will walk you through the entire process, ensuring that you have a thorough understanding of the requirements and procedures involved.

Starting a tax-exempt non-profit organization can be a complex journey, but with the right knowledge and guidance, you can navigate the process successfully. By understanding the fundamentals of non-profit organizations and the steps to obtain tax-exempt status, you will be well-equipped to make a positive and lasting impact in your community.

Whether you are passionate about education, healthcare, environmental conservation, or any other cause, this subchapter will provide you with the essential knowledge and resources to turn your idea into a tax-exempt non-profit organization.

Benefits of Starting a Non-Profit

Starting a non-profit organization can be a fulfilling and impactful endeavor. Whether you have a burning passion for a cause or want to create positive change in your community, a non-profit can be the perfect platform to make a difference. In this subchapter, we will explore the numerous benefits of starting a non-profit and how it can be a rewarding journey for anyone who wants to make a difference.

One of the primary benefits of starting a non-profit is the ability to create meaningful change in society. Non-profits provide a platform to address pressing social issues, advocate for marginalized communities, promote the arts, support education, and much more. By starting a non-profit, you have the opportunity to build a team of like-minded individuals who share your vision and work towards a common goal.

Another significant advantage of starting a non-profit is the ability to inspire and mobilize others. When you are passionate about a cause, it is contagious, and others are often eager to support your mission. By establishing a non-profit, you can engage volunteers, donors, and community members who are passionate about your cause. Their involvement can greatly amplify the impact of your organization and help you achieve your goals.

Furthermore, starting a non-profit can provide personal and professional growth opportunities. As a founder, you will gain valuable leadership skills, learn to manage teams, develop fundraising strategies, and navigate complex legal and financial processes. These experiences can be invaluable, whether you choose to continue working in the non-profit sector or pursue other career paths.

One of the unique benefits of starting a tax-exempt non-profit is the ability to receive financial support through grants and donations. By obtaining tax-exempt status, your organization becomes eligible for various funding opportunities from government agencies, foundations, and individual donors. This financial support can help sustain your operations, expand your programs, and ultimately make a greater impact.

Finally, starting a non-profit allows you to build a legacy. By establishing an organization that will continue to exist beyond your lifetime, you can leave a lasting impact on your community and the causes you care about. Your non-profit can become a beacon of hope and a catalyst for change, creating a positive ripple effect for generations to come.

In conclusion, starting a non-profit organization offers numerous benefits, from creating meaningful change to personal and professional growth. By following this step-by-step guide on filing tax-exempt status for non-profit organizations, you will be equipped with the knowledge and tools necessary to embark on this rewarding journey. Remember, anyone who wants to make a difference can start a non-profit and contribute to a better world.

Challenges and Considerations

Starting a non-profit organization can be an incredibly rewarding and fulfilling experience. However, it is important to be aware of the challenges and considerations that come along with this endeavor. In this subchapter, we will explore some of the key obstacles you may encounter and provide guidance on how to navigate them successfully.

One of the primary challenges you may face is the complex process of filing for tax-exempt status. The Internal Revenue Service (IRS) has specific requirements and guidelines that must be met for a non-profit organization to qualify for tax exemption. Navigating this process can be time-consuming and overwhelming, especially for individuals who are not familiar with the intricacies of tax law. However, with careful planning and attention to detail, it is possible to successfully file for tax-exempt status.

Another consideration is the financial sustainability of your non-profit organization. Many non-profits struggle to secure ongoing funding to support their programs and initiatives. It is essential to develop a comprehensive fundraising strategy that includes diverse revenue streams, such as grants, individual donations, and corporate sponsorships. Additionally, it is crucial to create a robust budget that accurately reflects the organization's expenses and income projections.

Building a strong and committed board of directors is also a critical consideration. Your board members will play a crucial role in guiding and supporting your non-profit organization. Selecting individuals with diverse backgrounds, expertise, and a passion for your mission is essential. It is also important to establish clear expectations and roles for board members to ensure effective governance and decision-making.

Lastly, it is essential to consider the long-term sustainability and impact of your non-profit organization. Developing a strategic plan that outlines your goals, objectives, and the steps needed to achieve them is vital. Regularly evaluating and reassessing your organization's progress and impact will allow you to make necessary adjustments and improvements.

Starting a tax-exempt non-profit organization comes with its own set of challenges and considerations. However, with careful planning, diligent research, and a commitment to your mission, you can overcome these obstacles and create a successful and impactful organization. This subchapter has provided an overview of some of the key challenges and considerations you may encounter along the way. By proactively addressing these issues, you will be better prepared to navigate the path from idea to exemption.

Chapter 2: Developing Your Non-Profit Idea

Identifying Your Mission and Vision

When starting a non-profit organization, it is crucial to clearly define your mission and vision. These foundational elements will guide your organization's activities, strategies, and decision-making processes. In this subchapter, we will explore the importance of identifying your mission and vision and provide step-by-step guidance on how to develop them effectively.

Your mission statement is a concise declaration of your organization's purpose and the reason it exists. It should encapsulate the core values and principles that drive your non-profit. A strong mission statement serves as a compass, ensuring that all activities align with your organization's overall objectives. It also helps potential donors, volunteers, and stakeholders understand what you aim to achieve.

To develop an effective mission statement, start by reflecting on the problem or issue your non-profit wants to address. Consider the needs of your target audience or the community you aim to serve. Ask yourself, "What impact do I want to make?" and "How can my non-profit contribute to positive change?"

Once you have a clear understanding of your mission, it's time to craft a vision statement. While the mission statement focuses on the present, the vision statement looks into the future. It articulates your desired long-term impact and sets the direction for your non-profit's growth and development.

When creating a vision statement, think big and be aspirational. Envision the ultimate outcome you want to achieve, without getting caught up in the specifics of how to get there. Your vision statement should inspire and motivate both your team and potential supporters.

To ensure that your mission and vision statements accurately reflect your non-profit's goals, engage in a collaborative process. Involve key stakeholders, board members, and volunteers in brainstorming sessions and discussions. Their input can provide valuable perspectives and help refine your organization's purpose.

Remember that your mission and vision statements are not set in stone. As your non-profit evolves, you may need to revisit and revise them. Regularly reassessing your mission and vision ensures they remain relevant and aligned with your organization's goals.

In conclusion, identifying your mission and vision is a crucial step in starting a non-profit organization. These statements serve as guiding principles and help convey your purpose to stakeholders. By carefully crafting your mission and vision, you lay the foundation for a successful and impactful non-profit organization.

Defining Your Target Audience

In the world of non-profit organizations, understanding and defining your target audience is crucial for success. Your target audience consists of the specific group of people or organizations that your non-profit aims to serve, and it forms the foundation for all your future efforts. By identifying and understanding your target audience, you can tailor your programs, services, and messaging to effectively meet their needs and achieve your organization's mission.

When it comes to starting a tax-exempt non-profit organization, defining your target audience is even more crucial. This subchapter will guide you through the process of identifying your target audience, ensuring that your efforts are focused and impactful.

To begin, consider the mission and goals of your non-profit. What social or community issue are you aiming to address? Whether it's education, healthcare, environmental conservation, or any other cause, understanding the specific problem you want to solve will help you narrow down your target audience.

Next, ask yourself who is most affected by this issue. Who are the individuals or groups that would benefit the most from your organization's services or programs? Consider demographics such as age, gender, location, and socioeconomic status. Understanding these characteristics will help you tailor your offerings to meet their unique needs.

Alongside demographics, it's important to consider psychographics as well. Psychographics involve understanding the attitudes, interests, values, and behaviors of your target audience. What are their motivations and aspirations? What challenges do they face, and what solutions are they seeking? By delving deeper into their psychographics, you can better connect with your target audience on an emotional level and position your non-profit as a solution provider.

Additionally, it's essential to analyze the existing non-profit landscape in your niche. Identify other organizations that are working towards similar goals or serving a similar audience. This will help you identify any gaps in services and differentiate your non-profit by focusing on underserved areas or unique approaches.

Once you have defined your target audience, it's important to continuously evaluate and refine your understanding. As your organization grows and evolves, so may the needs and preferences of your audience. Regularly collecting feedback, conducting surveys, and staying engaged with your target audience will ensure that you stay aligned with their evolving needs and maintain a strong connection.

Defining your target audience is the first step in building a successful tax-exempt non-profit organization. By understanding who you aim to serve and tailoring your efforts to meet their needs, you can make a significant impact in your chosen niche.

Conducting Market Research

Before starting a non-profit organization, it is crucial to conduct thorough market research to ensure the viability and success of your venture. Market research will provide valuable insights into the needs and preferences of your target audience, help you identify potential competitors, and guide your decision-making process.

Understanding your target audience is fundamental to the success of your non-profit organization. Conducting market research will help you identify the specific needs, interests, and challenges of the individuals or communities you aim to serve. By gathering demographic information, such as age, gender, location, and socioeconomic status, you can develop programs and services that are tailored to their unique circumstances. Additionally, market research can help you determine the best channels and methods for reaching your target audience, ensuring that your message effectively reaches those who need it most.

Market research will also enable you to identify potential competitors in the non-profit sector. By analyzing existing organizations providing similar services or addressing similar causes, you can learn from their strategies and differentiate your own organization. This knowledge will allow you to develop a unique value proposition that sets your non-profit apart and attracts supporters, volunteers, and funding.

There are various methods and tools available for conducting market research. Surveys, focus groups, and interviews can provide direct insights from your target audience, while online research, social media monitoring, and data analysis can offer valuable information about industry trends, donor behavior, and potential funding sources. It is important to utilize a combination of qualitative and quantitative research methods to obtain a comprehensive understanding of your market.

Once you have gathered and analyzed the data from your market research, it is essential to incorporate these findings into your strategic planning and decision-making processes. By aligning your organization's mission, goals, and activities with the needs and preferences of your target audience, you can increase the likelihood of achieving your desired impact and securing tax-exempt status.

In conclusion, conducting market research is a vital step in starting a non-profit organization. It allows you to gain insights into your target audience, identify potential competitors, and make informed decisions. By understanding the market landscape, you can develop a strategic plan that maximizes your organization's potential for success. Remember, market research is an ongoing process, and it is crucial to regularly reassess and adapt your strategies based on new data and changing market dynamics.

Chapter 3: Building Your Non-Profit Team

Assembling a Board of Directors

One of the most crucial steps in starting a non-profit organization is assembling a strong and dedicated Board of Directors. The Board will play a vital role in the success and growth of your organization, and their expertise and guidance will be invaluable as you navigate the process of obtaining tax-exempt status. In this subchapter, we will provide a step-by-step guide on how to effectively assemble a Board of Directors for your non-profit organization.

The first step is to identify individuals who share your passion and vision for the cause your non-profit aims to address. Look for individuals with diverse backgrounds and skill sets, as this will ensure a well-rounded board capable of providing sound advice and making informed decisions. Consider reaching out to professionals in the field, community leaders, and individuals who have experience with non-profit organizations.

Once you have identified potential board members, it is important to communicate your organization's mission and goals to them. Share your vision and explain how their involvement can make a significant impact. This will help attract individuals who are genuinely interested in furthering your cause.

Next, create a clear and concise job description outlining the roles and responsibilities of board members. This will ensure that potential candidates understand what is expected of them and can make an informed decision about joining your board. Be sure to emphasize the time commitment required, as serving on a board can be demanding.

When interviewing potential board members, ask questions that assess their commitment, expertise, and compatibility with the organization's values. Look for individuals who are willing to actively contribute, bring new perspectives, and work collaboratively with other board members.

Once you have selected your board members, it is essential to establish clear expectations and policies. Develop a code of conduct that outlines ethical and professional behavior, as well as conflict of interest policies. Additionally, establish a process for board member recruitment, orientation, and ongoing training to ensure that your board remains effective and engaged.

In conclusion, assembling a Board of Directors is a critical step in starting a non-profit organization. By following these steps and selecting dedicated individuals who share your passion, you will build a strong and effective board that can help you navigate the process of obtaining tax-exempt status and drive the success of your organization.

Recruiting Volunteers and Staff Members

When starting a non-profit organization, one of the most crucial steps is finding dedicated and passionate individuals to join your cause as volunteers and staff members. Building a strong team is essential for the success of your organization, as they will be the driving force behind its mission and goals. In this subchapter, we will provide you with a step-by-step guide on how to effectively recruit volunteers and staff members for your tax-exempt non-profit organization.

1. Define your needs: Before launching a recruitment campaign, take the time to clearly define the roles and responsibilities you need to fill. Identify the skills, experience, and qualifications required for each position.

2. Develop compelling messaging: Craft a powerful mission statement and value proposition that resonates with potential volunteers and staff members. Clearly communicate the impact they can make by joining your organization.

3. Leverage your network: Start by reaching out to your personal and professional networks. Share your organization's vision and goals with friends, family, colleagues, and contacts in the non-profit sector. Ask for referrals and recommendations to expand your reach.

4. Utilize online platforms: Leverage social media platforms, such as Facebook, Twitter, and LinkedIn, to spread the word about your organization's mission and recruit volunteers and staff members. Create engaging content and share success stories to attract like-minded individuals.

5. Collaborate with local colleges and universities: Reach out to academic institutions in your area to establish partnerships and seek volunteers and interns. Many students are eager to gain hands-on experience and contribute to meaningful causes.

6. Attend community events and job fairs: Participate in local community events, job fairs, and career expos to connect with potential volunteers and staff members. Set up a booth and engage attendees with your organization's mission.

7. Host information sessions and orientation programs: Organize information sessions to provide potential recruits with an in-depth understanding of your organization's goals, programs, and volunteer opportunities. Conduct orientation programs to onboard new staff members effectively.

8. Recognize and appreciate your team: Show gratitude and appreciation for the contributions of your volunteers and staff members. Recognize their efforts publicly, provide training and skill development opportunities, and create a positive work environment.

Remember, building a strong team takes time and effort. Be patient, maintain open communication, and continuously evaluate the needs of your organization to recruit the best-fit individuals. By following these steps, you will be well on your way to assembling a dedicated and motivated team that will help your tax-exempt non-profit organization thrive.

Establishing Roles and Responsibilities

When starting a non-profit organization, one of the key steps is to establish clear roles and responsibilities for your team members. This subchapter will guide you through the process of defining these roles and ensuring that each team member understands their responsibilities. By doing so, you will create a strong foundation for your organization to thrive and achieve its mission.

1. Identifying Key Positions:
Begin by identifying the key positions required for the successful functioning of your non-profit. These positions may include a board of directors, executive director, program managers, volunteers, and various administrative roles. Each position should have a clear purpose and set of responsibilities.

2. Defining Roles and Responsibilities:
Once the key positions are identified, it is crucial to define the roles and responsibilities associated with each. This involves outlining the primary tasks and functions that each position is responsible for. For example, the board of directors may be responsible for setting the organization's strategic direction, while program managers oversee the implementation of specific programs.

3. Board of Directors:
The board of directors plays a critical role in the governance and decision-making process of a non-profit organization. This section will outline the responsibilities of board members, including fiduciary duties, fundraising, strategic planning, and ensuring compliance with legal and ethical standards.

4. Executive Director:
The executive director is responsible for the day-to-day operations of the organization. This section will discuss the qualifications and responsibilities of the executive director, including managing staff and volunteers, overseeing financial management, and representing the organization to stakeholders.

5. Staff and Volunteers:
In this section, we will explore the roles and responsibilities of staff members and volunteers. This includes recruitment and selection procedures, training and development, and fostering a positive work environment. Additionally, we will highlight the importance of clearly defining volunteer positions and ensuring they align with the organization's overall goals.

6. Organizational Structure:
The final part of this subchapter will address the importance of

establishing a clear organizational structure. This includes defining reporting relationships, communication channels, and decision-making processes. A well-defined structure helps ensure accountability and promotes efficient operations within the organization.

By establishing clear roles and responsibilities within your non-profit organization, you will cultivate a sense of purpose and direction among your team members. This subchapter provides a step-by-step guide on how to define and communicate these roles effectively. When everyone understands their responsibilities, your organization will be better equipped to achieve its mission and make a positive impact in the community.

Chapter 4: Creating Your Non-Profit Business Plan

Components of a Non-Profit Business Plan

A well-crafted business plan is essential for the success of any non-profit organization. It serves as a roadmap, outlining the organization's goals, strategies, and financial projections. In this subchapter, we will delve into the key components that should be included in a non-profit business plan.

1. Executive Summary: This section provides a concise overview of the entire business plan. It should capture the reader's attention and highlight the organization's mission, vision, and core values.

2. Organization Description: Here, you will provide detailed information about your non-profit organization. Explain its purpose, history, and the problem it aims to solve. Include the organization's legal structure, leadership team, and key staff members.

3. Mission and Vision Statements: Clearly articulate the organization's mission and vision. The mission statement should define the organization's purpose and the impact it seeks to make. The vision statement should outline the desired future state of the organization.

4. Programs and Services: Describe the programs and services your organization will offer to fulfill its mission. Explain how these initiatives will address the identified problem and benefit the target beneficiaries. Include details such as program goals, target population, and anticipated outcomes.

5. Marketing and Fundraising Strategy: Outline your organization's marketing and fundraising plans. Identify your target audience and detail how you will reach and engage them. Describe your fundraising strategies, including events, grants, and partnerships, to secure the necessary resources to support your programs.

6. Organizational Structure and Governance: Provide an overview of your organization's structure, including the board of directors, key staff, and volunteers. Explain how decisions are made and how the organization will be governed. Highlight any policies or procedures that ensure transparency and accountability.

7. Financial Projections: Present a detailed budget that outlines your projected income and expenses over the next three to five years. Include information on funding sources, such as grants, donations, and earned income. This section should also include financial statements, such as balance sheets and cash flow statements.

8. Evaluation and Impact Measurement: Describe how your organization will measure the impact of its programs and services. Explain the evaluation methods you will use to assess the effectiveness and success of your initiatives. This will help you demonstrate your organization's impact to potential funders and stakeholders.

Remember, a non-profit business plan is a living document that should be regularly reviewed and updated. It serves as a guide for your organization's growth and development, providing a framework for decision-making and resource allocation. By including these key components, you will create a comprehensive business plan that sets your non-profit organization on the path to success.

Setting Goals and Objectives

Setting clear and achievable goals and objectives is an essential step in starting a tax-exempt non-profit organization. It provides a roadmap for success and serves as a guiding principle for the organization's activities and decision-making processes. In this subchapter, we will delve into the importance of setting goals and objectives and provide you with a step-by-step guide on how to do so effectively.

Why are Goals and Objectives Important?

Goals and objectives give your non-profit organization direction, purpose, and focus. They provide a clear vision of what you want to achieve and help you outline the steps needed to get there. By setting goals and objectives, you create a framework that allows you to measure your progress and evaluate your success. Moreover, goals and objectives can inspire and motivate both your team members and potential donors.

Step-by-Step Guide to Setting Goals and Objectives

1. Identify your mission and vision: Before setting goals and objectives, it's crucial to have a clear understanding of your organization's mission and vision. What are you hoping to accomplish? What is your long-term vision for the non-profit? Defining these elements will help shape your goals and objectives.

2. Conduct a SWOT analysis: Assess your organization's strengths, weaknesses, opportunities, and threats (SWOT). This analysis will help you identify areas for improvement, potential challenges, and opportunities for growth. It will inform your goal-setting process.

3. Prioritize goals: Once you have conducted a SWOT analysis, prioritize the goals you wish to achieve. Consider the resources available, the level of importance, and the feasibility of each goal. Focus on those goals that align with your mission and have the potential for significant impact.

4. Make goals specific, measurable, attainable, relevant, and time-bound (SMART): Ensure that each goal is specific, measurable, attainable, relevant, and time-bound. For example, instead of setting a vague goal like "increase funding," make it more specific by stating "raise $50,000 in donations by the end of the year."

5. Break goals into objectives: Break down each goal into smaller, actionable objectives. Objectives should be concrete and measurable steps that contribute to achieving the overall goal. Assign responsibilities and deadlines to each objective.

6. Monitor and evaluate progress: Regularly monitor and evaluate your progress towards your goals and objectives. This will help you identify any necessary adjustments or modifications to stay on track.

By following these steps and setting clear goals and objectives, you will significantly increase your non-profit organization's chances of success. Remember, goals and objectives provide a roadmap for your organization, keeping you focused and motivated as you work towards achieving your mission and making a positive impact in your community.

Developing a Fundraising Strategy

When starting a non-profit organization, one of the key elements to ensure its sustainability and success is developing a fundraising strategy. Fundraising is essential to secure the financial resources needed to support the organization's mission and activities. In this subchapter, we will guide you through the process of creating an effective fundraising strategy that will help you achieve your goals.

1. Identify Your Funding Needs: Start by assessing your organization's financial requirements. Determine the amount of funds needed to support your programs, cover operating expenses, and achieve long-term goals. This will provide you with a clear understanding of the fundraising targets you need to set.

2. Define Your Target Donors: Identify the individuals, foundations, corporations, and government entities that are most likely to support your cause. Consider their motivations, interests, and giving capacity. This will help you tailor your fundraising efforts to appeal to potential donors effectively.

3. Diversify Your Funding Sources: It is crucial to establish a diversified funding base to reduce dependence on a single source. Explore various fundraising avenues such as individual donations, grants, corporate sponsorships, fundraising events, and partnerships. By diversifying your funding sources, you can mitigate financial risks and increase your chances of securing sustainable support.

4. Craft Your Fundraising Message: Develop a compelling and concise message that clearly communicates your organization's mission, impact, and the importance of donors' contributions. Highlight the unique aspects of your non-profit and how it addresses a pressing need in your community. Tailor your message to resonate with each donor segment you are targeting.

5. Create a Fundraising Plan: Outline your fundraising goals and the specific strategies and tactics you will employ to achieve them. Set clear timelines, budgetary requirements, and measurable objectives. Your fundraising plan should include details on donor cultivation, stewardship, and acknowledgement strategies.

6. Leverage Technology and Social Media: In today's digital age, utilizing technology and social media platforms is essential for successful fundraising. Establish an online presence through a website and social media channels to connect with potential donors, share your impact stories, and facilitate online donations. Explore crowdfunding platforms to expand your fundraising reach.

7. Evaluate and Adapt: Regularly assess the effectiveness of your fundraising efforts. Analyze which strategies are generating the desired results and adjust your approach accordingly. Pay attention to donor feedback and engagement levels to refine your fundraising techniques continually.

By developing a comprehensive fundraising strategy, you will be better equipped to secure the necessary financial support to fulfill your non-profit organization's mission. Remember, fundraising is an ongoing process that requires dedication, creativity, and adaptability. With a well-crafted plan and a committed team, you can successfully raise funds and make a meaningful impact in your community.

Chapter 5: Legal Requirements for Non-Profit Organizations

Choosing a Legal Structure

When starting a tax-exempt non-profit organization, one of the most crucial decisions you will face is choosing the right legal structure. The legal structure you select will have far-reaching implications for your organization's governance, tax obligations, and liability. This subchapter will provide you with a step-by-step guide on choosing the appropriate legal structure for your non-profit organization.

There are several common legal structures for non-profit organizations, including charitable trusts, unincorporated associations, and non-profit corporations. Each structure has its own advantages and disadvantages, so it is essential to carefully consider your organization's specific needs and goals.

Charitable trusts are a suitable option for those who want to establish a non-profit organization to manage and distribute funds for charitable purposes. While they offer flexibility and autonomy, they also come with increased administrative burdens and limited public visibility.

Unincorporated associations, on the other hand, are simple and cost-effective structures for smaller non-profit organizations. However, they provide less legal protection and may face challenges when it comes to obtaining grants or entering into contracts.

Non-profit corporations are the most common and widely recognized legal structure for non-profit organizations. They offer limited liability protection for board members and can engage in a broad range of activities. Non-profit corporations also provide credibility and transparency, which are essential for attracting donors and securing grants.

To choose the most suitable legal structure, consider factors such as your organization's size, mission, funding requirements, and long-term goals. Additionally, consult with legal professionals who specialize in non-profit law to ensure compliance with state and federal regulations.

Once you have identified the ideal legal structure, you will need to file the necessary paperwork with the appropriate governmental agencies. This typically involves drafting articles of incorporation, bylaws, and other organizational documents. It is crucial to carefully review and follow all filing requirements to ensure a smooth and successful application for tax-exempt status.

Remember, choosing the right legal structure is a critical decision that will impact your organization's future. Take the time to research, seek expert advice, and carefully consider the pros and cons of each option. By selecting the appropriate legal structure, you will lay a solid foundation for your non-profit organization's success and make the journey towards tax-exempt status smoother and more efficient.

Registering Your Non-Profit

Registering Your Non-Profit: A Step-by-Step Guide to Filing for Tax-Exempt Status

Introduction:
Starting a non-profit organization is a noble endeavor that can make a meaningful impact in your community or the world at large. However, before you can begin carrying out your mission, it is essential to

navigate the process of registering your non-profit and obtaining tax-exempt status. This subchapter will provide you with a comprehensive step-by-step guide on how to file for tax-exempt status for your non-profit organization.

Understanding the Importance of Tax-Exempt Status:
Tax-exempt status is crucial for non-profit organizations as it allows them to receive tax-deductible donations, apply for grants, and enjoy certain exemptions from federal and state taxes. By registering your non-profit and obtaining tax-exempt status, you can maximize your organization's financial resources and credibility.

Step 1: Research and Planning:
Before diving into the registration process, take the time to research and plan your non-profit organization thoroughly. Define your mission, develop a strategic plan, and determine the specific services or programs you will offer. This groundwork will help you gather the necessary information for the registration process.

Step 2: Choose a Legal Structure:
Selecting the appropriate legal structure for your non-profit is essential. The most common options include a charitable trust, unincorporated association, or incorporating as a nonprofit corporation. Each structure has its own advantages and requirements, so carefully evaluate which option aligns best with your organization's goals.

Step 3: Name Your Non-Profit:
Choosing a name that reflects your mission and is unique is crucial. Research existing non-profit names to avoid conflicts and consider trademark protection. Check your state's naming requirements and ensure the chosen name complies with the Internal Revenue Service (IRS) guidelines.

Step 4: Draft Your Articles of Incorporation:
If you decide to incorporate as a nonprofit corporation, drafting your articles of incorporation is necessary. This legal document outlines your organization's purpose, structure, and governance. Seek legal advice to ensure compliance with state laws and IRS requirements.

Step 5: Obtain an Employer Identification Number (EIN):
An EIN is a unique number assigned by the IRS to identify your non-profit organization for tax purposes. Apply for an EIN through the IRS website or by mail using Form SS-4.

Step 6: Prepare and File Form 1023 or 1023-EZ:
Form 1023 or 1023-EZ is the application for tax-exempt status. Depending on your organization's size and projected revenue, you may qualify for the streamlined 1023-EZ form. These forms require detailed information about your organization, including its purpose, activities, governance structure, and financial data. Complete the form accurately and attach any necessary supporting documents.

Step 7: Pay the Required Filing Fee:
When submitting your application, you must include the appropriate filing fee. The fee amount depends on your organization's projected revenue and can be found on the IRS website.

Step 8: Await IRS Determination:
After submitting your application, the IRS will review it and determine your organization's eligibility for tax-exempt status. This process may take several weeks or months. Be patient and prepare to respond promptly to any additional information requested by the IRS.

Conclusion:
Registering your non-profit and obtaining tax-exempt status is a critical

step towards establishing a successful organization. By following this step-by-step guide, you can navigate the registration process with confidence and ensure that your non-profit is positioned to make a lasting impact in your community. Remember, seeking professional advice from attorneys or tax experts experienced in non-profit law can provide invaluable guidance throughout this process.

Understanding Tax-Exempt Status

Starting a non-profit organization can be a fulfilling and impactful endeavor. However, navigating the complexities of tax-exempt status can often seem daunting. Fortunately, with the right knowledge and guidance, obtaining tax-exempt status for your non-profit can be a smooth and successful process. This subchapter aims to provide a comprehensive understanding of tax-exempt status and serve as a step-by-step guide for filing it.

Before delving into the intricacies of tax-exempt status, it is important to grasp its significance. Tax-exempt status refers to the privilege granted by the government to certain organizations that allows them to be exempt from paying federal income tax. This status is crucial for non-profit organizations as it enables them to allocate resources towards their mission, rather than being burdened by excessive taxes.

To start the process of filing for tax-exempt status, it is crucial to understand the different types of non-profit organizations that qualify. These include charitable, religious, educational, scientific, literary, and more. Each type has specific requirements and benefits, so it is essential to determine the most suitable designation for your organization.

Next, you will need to gather the necessary documents and information for your application. This includes drafting a mission statement, creating bylaws, and developing a strategic plan. Additionally, you will need to compile financial statements, a budget, and a description of your programs and activities. It is advisable to consult legal and tax professionals to ensure accuracy and compliance throughout this process.

Once all the required documents have been prepared, you can submit your application to the Internal Revenue Service (IRS). The application, known as Form 1023, requires detailed information about your organization, its activities, finances, and governance structure. It is crucial to complete this form accurately and provide all requested information to avoid delays or potential rejections.

After submitting your application, it is essential to be patient as the IRS reviews it. The processing time may vary, but it is advisable to periodically check the status of your application to address any potential issues promptly. Once approved, you will receive a determination letter from the IRS, officially granting tax-exempt status to your organization.

Understanding tax-exempt status is vital for anyone who wants to start a non-profit organization. This subchapter has provided a step-by-step guide for filing tax-exempt status, ensuring that your organization can maximize its impact and resources. By obtaining tax-exempt status, you will be able to focus on your mission and make a lasting difference in your community and beyond.

Chapter 6: Understanding Tax-Exempt Status

Overview of Tax-Exempt Status

Eligibility Criteria for Tax-Exempt Status

When starting a non-profit organization, one of the most important steps is to secure tax-exempt status. This status allows your organization to operate without paying federal income tax, making it an essential aspect of running a successful non-profit. To help you navigate this process, this subchapter will provide a comprehensive overview of the eligibility criteria for tax-exempt status.

To qualify for tax-exempt status, your non-profit organization must meet certain requirements set forth by the Internal Revenue Service (IRS). The primary criterion is that your organization must be organized and operated exclusively for charitable, educational, religious, scientific, or other specified purposes. These purposes must fall under the categories defined by the IRS, such as promoting social welfare or advancing the arts.

Additionally, your non-profit must demonstrate that it will not be operated for the benefit of any private individual or shareholder. This means that the organization's activities and funds should be used for the betterment of the community or the specific cause it aims to address.

The IRS also requires that your non-profit's assets and earnings cannot be used to personally benefit any individual or group of individuals. Instead, any income generated should be reinvested back into the organization to further its mission and objectives. This ensures that the non-profit remains dedicated to its charitable purposes rather than being exploited for personal gain.

Furthermore, your non-profit must adhere to certain limitations and restrictions on lobbying and political activities. While non-profits are allowed to engage in some advocacy work, the IRS has specific guidelines to prevent excessive political involvement. Understanding and following these limitations is crucial to maintaining tax-exempt status.

Finally, it is essential to note that obtaining tax-exempt status requires proper documentation and filing with the IRS. This process involves completing Form 1023, the Application for Recognition of Exemption Under Section 501(c)(3) of the Internal Revenue Code. The form requires detailed information about your organization's structure, activities, and financials.

To assist you in filing for tax-exempt status, the subsequent chapters of this book will provide a step-by-step guide, explaining each section of Form 1023 and offering valuable tips and insights. By following this comprehensive guide, you will increase your chances of obtaining tax-exempt status, allowing your non-profit organization to thrive and make a difference in your chosen field.

In conclusion, understanding the eligibility criteria for tax-exempt status is crucial for anyone looking to start a non-profit organization. By meeting the IRS requirements and completing the necessary application process, you can secure tax-exempt status and lay a solid foundation for your non-profit's success.

Benefits and Limitations of Tax-Exemption

Starting a non-profit organization can be a rewarding endeavor, but it also comes with its fair share of challenges. One crucial aspect that every aspiring non-profit founder must consider is the tax-exempt status. This subchapter will delve into the benefits and limitations of tax-exemption, providing you with a comprehensive understanding of its implications for your non-profit organization.

Benefits:

1. Tax savings: Perhaps the most significant advantage of obtaining tax-exempt status is the potential for substantial tax savings. As a tax-exempt non-profit, your organization will be exempt from federal income tax, as well as certain state and local taxes. This can free up a significant portion of your budget, allowing you to allocate more resources to your mission and programs.

2. Eligibility for grants and donations: Many foundations, corporations, and individuals prefer to donate to tax-exempt organizations as their contributions may be tax-deductible. By obtaining tax-exempt status, you open the door to a wider range of funding opportunities, including grants and tax-deductible donations, which can help sustain and expand your organization's impact.

3. Credibility and trust: Tax-exempt status provides your organization with a higher level of credibility and legitimacy in the eyes of potential donors, volunteers, and stakeholders. It demonstrates that your organization has undergone a rigorous vetting process and adheres to strict compliance standards. This can foster trust and enhance your

organization's reputation, making it more attractive to supporters and beneficiaries.

Limitations:

1. Restrictions on political activities: One crucial limitation of tax-exempt status is the restriction on engaging in certain political activities. Non-profit organizations are prohibited from endorsing or opposing political candidates or participating in partisan activities. This limitation ensures that non-profit organizations remain focused on their charitable mission rather than becoming entangled in political controversies.

2. Reporting and transparency requirements: Obtaining tax-exempt status comes with a set of reporting obligations. Non-profit organizations are required to file annual information returns with the IRS, providing details about their financial activities and operations. This transparency ensures accountability and helps maintain the public's trust. However, it does add an additional administrative burden on your organization, requiring careful record-keeping and compliance with reporting deadlines.

3. Limited income-generating activities: While non-profit organizations can engage in some income-generating activities, such as selling merchandise or charging fees for services, these activities should be related to the organization's mission. Non-profits cannot engage in significant commercial activities that generate unrelated business income, as this could jeopardize their tax-exempt status.

Understanding the benefits and limitations of tax-exemption is crucial for anyone starting a non-profit organization. It allows you to weigh the advantages against the constraints and make informed decisions regarding your organization's structure and goals. By navigating the complexities of tax-exempt status effectively, you can position your non-profit for long-term success and maximize its impact in the community.

Chapter 7: Step-by-Step Guide to Filing for Tax-Exempt Status

Preparing the Application

When it comes to starting a tax-exempt non-profit organization, one of the most crucial steps is preparing the application for tax-exempt status. This subchapter will provide you with a comprehensive step-by-step guide on how to file for tax-exempt status, ensuring that your organization meets all the necessary requirements.

Before you begin the application process, it's essential to have a clear understanding of your organization's mission, goals, and activities. This will help you determine the appropriate tax-exempt status to pursue, whether it's a 501(c)(3) for charitable organizations, a 501(c)(4) for social welfare organizations, or another applicable category.

The first step in preparing the application is gathering all the necessary information and documentation. This includes your organization's articles of incorporation, bylaws, financial statements, budget, and any other supporting documents required by the IRS. It's important to ensure that these documents are accurate, complete, and well-organized to facilitate the application process.

Next, you will need to complete Form 1023 or Form 1023-EZ, depending on the size and nature of your organization. These forms require detailed information about your organization's activities, governance structure, financial operations, and more. It's crucial to answer all questions accurately and provide supporting evidence where required.

In addition to the application forms, you will also need to prepare a narrative description of your organization's mission and activities. This is an opportunity to showcase the impact your non-profit aims to make and highlight the need for tax-exempt status. It's important to be clear, concise, and compelling in your narrative, as it can greatly influence the approval process.

Once you have completed the application and reviewed it thoroughly, it's time to submit it to the IRS. It's essential to keep copies of all documents and communications related to your application for future reference. The processing time for tax-exempt status applications can vary, so it's important to be patient and follow up with the IRS if necessary.

In conclusion, preparing the application for tax-exempt status is a critical step in starting a non-profit organization. By following this step-by-step guide and ensuring that all necessary information and documentation are provided, you can increase the likelihood of a successful application. Remember to be thorough, accurate, and compelling in your application to demonstrate your organization's eligibility for tax-exempt status.

Completing Form 1023 or 1023-EZ

If you are considering starting a non-profit organization, one of the most critical steps you need to take is obtaining tax-exempt status. This allows your organization to receive tax-deductible donations and grants, ensuring financial stability and legitimacy. To achieve this status, you will need to complete either Form 1023 or 1023-EZ, depending on the size and complexity of your organization.

Form 1023 is the standard application for recognition of exemption under section 501(c)(3) of the Internal Revenue Code. It is a comprehensive and detailed form that requires substantial documentation and information about your organization's mission, activities, governance structure, and financials. This form is typically recommended for organizations with significant revenues and complex operations.

On the other hand, Form 1023-EZ is a streamlined version of the standard form, designed for smaller organizations with less than $50,000 in annual gross receipts and $250,000 in total assets. This form requires less documentation and is generally quicker to complete. However, it is essential to note that not all organizations are eligible for the simplified form, so it's crucial to review the eligibility requirements carefully.

To ensure a successful application process, it is highly recommended to follow a step-by-step guide. This subchapter will provide you with a comprehensive overview of the process involved in completing Form 1023 or 1023-EZ, including the necessary documentation, tips for answering questions accurately, and common mistakes to avoid.

First and foremost, it is crucial to thoroughly read and understand the instructions provided with the form. This will help you gather the necessary information and supporting documents before you begin filling out the form. It's also essential to double-check that you have selected the correct form based on your organization's size and complexity.

Next, we will guide you through each section of the form, explaining the purpose of the questions and providing tips on how to answer them accurately. We will discuss the key elements to include in your organization's mission statement, how to describe your activities and programs effectively, and the importance of providing clear and concise financial information.

Additionally, we will share insights into common mistakes made during the application process and provide guidance on how to avoid them. These may include incomplete or inconsistent answers, insufficient documentation, or overlooking important sections of the form.

By the end of this subchapter, you will have a clear understanding of the requirements and process involved in completing Form 1023 or 1023-EZ. Armed with this knowledge, you will be better prepared to navigate the application process and increase your chances of obtaining tax-exempt status for your non-profit organization.

Remember, starting a tax-exempt non-profit organization is a significant undertaking. It requires careful planning, attention to detail, and adherence to legal requirements. However, with the right guidance and knowledge, you can successfully navigate the process and establish a strong foundation for your organization's future success.

Required Attachments and Supporting Documents

When it comes to starting a tax-exempt non-profit organization, there are several crucial steps that need to be followed to ensure a successful application for tax-exempt status. One of these important steps is gathering and submitting the required attachments and supporting documents. In this subchapter, we will provide you with a step-by-step guide on the specific documents you need to include in your application, as well as their significance in obtaining tax-exempt status.

The Internal Revenue Service (IRS) requires certain attachments and supporting documents to be submitted along with your application for tax-exempt status. These documents help the IRS evaluate your organization's eligibility for tax-exempt status and ensure that you meet the necessary requirements. Here are the key attachments and supporting documents you will need to include:

1. Articles of Incorporation: This is a legal document that establishes your non-profit organization as a corporation. It includes important information such as the purpose of your organization, its name, and the names of its directors.

2. Bylaws: These are the rules and regulations that govern your organization's internal operations. Bylaws outline how your organization will be managed, including procedures for electing board members and making important decisions.

3. Financial Statements: You will need to prepare and submit financial statements that provide a clear picture of your organization's financial health. This may include balance sheets, income statements, and cash flow statements.

4. Budget: A budget is a financial plan that outlines your projected income and expenses for a specific period. Including a detailed budget demonstrates your organization's financial planning and sustainability.

5. Narrative Description of Activities: This document provides a comprehensive overview of your organization's mission, programs, and activities. It helps the IRS understand the purpose and impact of your non-profit organization.

6. Compensation Information: You will need to disclose the compensation and benefits provided to your organization's key employees and board members. This information ensures transparency and prevents excessive compensation.

7. Conflict of Interest Policy: A conflict of interest policy outlines how your organization will address potential conflicts of interest among its directors and key employees. This policy demonstrates your commitment to ethical practices.

8. Fundraising Materials: If your organization engages in fundraising activities, you may need to submit sample fundraising materials, such as brochures or solicitation letters, to showcase your fundraising strategies.

By including these attachments and supporting documents with your application, you provide the IRS with a comprehensive understanding of your organization's structure, activities, and financial management. This increases your chances of obtaining tax-exempt status and demonstrates your commitment to transparency and accountability.

Remember, it is important to carefully review the IRS guidelines and instructions for the specific attachments and supporting documents required for your application. By following these guidelines and providing accurate and complete information, you will be well on your way to starting a tax-exempt non-profit organization successfully.

In conclusion, the required attachments and supporting documents play a crucial role in the process of obtaining tax-exempt status for your non-profit organization. They provide the IRS with a comprehensive understanding of your organization's operations and financial management. By carefully preparing and submitting these documents, you demonstrate your organization's eligibility and commitment to transparency and accountability.

Chapter 8: Navigating the IRS Review Process

What to Expect After Submitting Your Application

Congratulations! You've taken the first step in starting your non-profit organization by submitting your application for tax-exempt status. This is an exciting milestone, but what happens next? In this subchapter, we will guide you through the process of what to expect after submitting your application.

Once your application is submitted, the Internal Revenue Service (IRS) will review it to determine if your organization meets the requirements for tax-exempt status. This review process can take several months, so it's important to be patient during this time. While waiting for a response, there are a few things you can do to stay proactive:

1. Maintain open lines of communication: It's crucial to keep the lines of communication open with the IRS. Make sure you have provided accurate contact information in your application and be prompt in responding to any requests for additional information.

2. Monitor your application status: The IRS provides an online tool called Exempt Organizations Select Check, which allows you to track the status of your application. Check this tool periodically to stay updated on the progress of your application.

3. Prepare for potential follow-up: It's not uncommon for the IRS to request additional information or clarification on certain aspects of your

application. Be prepared to provide any necessary documentation promptly to avoid delays in the review process.

4. Seek professional assistance if needed: If you encounter any challenges or have questions during this process, don't hesitate to seek professional assistance. Tax professionals or attorneys experienced in non-profit law can provide valuable guidance and support.

Once the IRS completes its review, you will receive a determination letter stating whether your organization has been granted tax-exempt status. This letter is a crucial document that verifies your organization's eligibility for tax benefits and allows you to solicit tax-deductible donations from supporters.

If your application is approved, congratulations! You can now focus on fulfilling your organization's mission and making a positive impact in your community. However, if your application is denied, don't be discouraged. The determination letter will explain the reasons for the denial, and you can choose to appeal the decision or make necessary changes to reapply.

In conclusion, the process of obtaining tax-exempt status for your non-profit organization may take time, but it is a crucial step in establishing your presence and credibility. By understanding what to expect after submitting your application, you can stay proactive and ensure a smooth and successful journey towards achieving your non-profit's goals.

Common Reasons for Application Rejection

When starting a non-profit organization, one of the most critical steps is obtaining tax-exempt status. However, the application process can be complex and rigorous. Many aspiring non-profit founders are unaware of the common reasons for application rejection, leading to frustration and delays. In this subchapter, we will explore the key factors that often lead to rejection and provide guidance on how to avoid them.

1. Incomplete or Inaccurate Documentation: One of the most common reasons for rejection is submitting incomplete or inaccurate documentation. The application requires detailed information about the organization's mission, activities, governance structure, and financial records. Failure to provide all the necessary documents or providing incorrect information can result in rejection. To avoid this, it is crucial to carefully review the application requirements and ensure that all documents are complete and accurate.

2. Lack of a Clear Charitable Purpose: To be eligible for tax-exempt status, a non-profit organization must have a clear charitable purpose. This purpose should be stated explicitly in the application and align with the Internal Revenue Service (IRS) guidelines. Rejection often occurs when the purpose is vague or does not meet the criteria for tax-exempt status. It is essential to clearly articulate the organization's mission and demonstrate how it benefits the public.

3. Inadequate Financial Documentation: The IRS requires non-profit organizations to provide detailed financial records to establish their financial stability and accountability. Failure to provide comprehensive financial documentation is a common reason for rejection. Applicants should include financial statements, budgets, and other relevant

documents to demonstrate the organization's ability to manage funds responsibly.

4. Lack of Proper Governance Structure: A non-profit organization must have a well-defined governance structure, including a board of directors and appropriate bylaws. Rejection can occur if the organization fails to demonstrate a proper governance structure or if the board of directors lacks independence or conflicts of interest are present. It is essential to establish a strong governance framework that complies with legal requirements.

5. Inconsistent or Insufficient Activities: The IRS expects non-profit organizations to engage in activities that align with their stated mission. Rejection can occur if the organization's activities are inconsistent or insufficient to fulfill their charitable purpose. Applicants should provide a detailed plan of activities and demonstrate how they will achieve their mission effectively.

By familiarizing yourself with these common reasons for application rejection, you can avoid unnecessary delays and increase your chances of obtaining tax-exempt status for your non-profit organization. It is crucial to carefully review the application requirements, provide accurate and complete documentation, and ensure that your organization's purpose, finances, governance, and activities align with the IRS guidelines. By doing so, you will be on the right path to successfully navigating the application process and establishing a tax-exempt non-profit organization.

Responding to IRS Inquiries or Requests for Additional Information

Once you have filed for tax-exempt status for your nonprofit organization, it is important to be prepared for the possibility of receiving inquiries or requests for additional information from the Internal Revenue Service (IRS). These inquiries may arise during the application process or even after your organization has been granted tax-exempt status. It is crucial to understand how to respond to these inquiries effectively and promptly to ensure the smooth operation and compliance of your nonprofit.

When you receive an inquiry or request for additional information from the IRS, it is important first to remain calm and not panic. The IRS may require additional details or clarification on certain aspects of your application or financial statements. Understanding this as a normal part of the process will help you approach the situation with confidence.

The first step is to carefully review the IRS inquiry or request. Take note of any specific questions or documents they are seeking. It is essential to thoroughly understand what the IRS is asking for before proceeding with your response.

Next, gather all relevant documents and records that pertain to the inquiry. This may include your initial application, financial statements, bylaws, or any other supporting documentation. Organize these documents in a clear and concise manner, making it easier for the IRS to review and understand your response.

Craft your response in a professional and concise manner. Address each question or request directly, providing clear and accurate information. It is crucial to be transparent and honest in your response, as any inconsistencies or inaccuracies could raise further concerns from the IRS.

Consider seeking professional assistance if you feel overwhelmed or unsure about how to respond. Enlisting the help of a tax professional or attorney experienced in nonprofit tax law can provide you with expert guidance and ensure that your response meets all necessary requirements.

Finally, submit your response to the IRS within the prescribed timeframe mentioned in the inquiry. Timely and thorough responses demonstrate your commitment to compliance and cooperation. Keep copies of all correspondence for your records.

By understanding how to respond effectively to IRS inquiries or requests for additional information, you can navigate the tax-exempt status application process with confidence. Remember, the goal is to establish and maintain a transparent and compliant nonprofit organization that can focus on its mission and make a positive impact in the community.

Chapter 9: Maintaining Tax-Exempt Status

Annual Reporting Requirements

Once your non-profit organization has obtained tax-exempt status, it is important to understand and fulfill the annual reporting requirements. These requirements ensure transparency and accountability, and they are necessary to maintain your organization's tax-exempt status. In this subchapter, we will guide you through the step-by-step process of fulfilling these reporting obligations.

The Internal Revenue Service (IRS) requires non-profit organizations to file an annual information return, Form 990, 990-EZ, or 990-N, depending on the organization's annual gross receipts. Form 990 is the most comprehensive return and is filed by organizations with gross receipts over $200,000 or total assets over $500,000. The simpler Form 990-EZ is for organizations with gross receipts under $200,000 and total assets under $500,000. Lastly, organizations with gross receipts under $50,000 can file the 990-N, also known as the e-Postcard.

The purpose of these forms is to provide the IRS and the public with detailed information about your organization's finances, activities, governance, and compliance with applicable laws and regulations. It is crucial to complete these forms accurately and in a timely manner to maintain your tax-exempt status.

In this subchapter, we will guide you through the process of gathering the necessary information, understanding the different sections of the Form 990, and completing the form correctly. We will also provide helpful tips and best practices to ensure that your annual reporting is accurate and transparent.

Additionally, we will discuss the importance of maintaining proper financial records and internal controls throughout the year. This will not only facilitate the preparation of your annual reports but also help you monitor and evaluate your organization's financial health and compliance with legal requirements.

Furthermore, we will explore the consequences of failing to meet the annual reporting requirements. Non-compliance can result in penalties, fines, or even the revocation of your organization's tax-exempt status. We will provide guidance on how to avoid these pitfalls and maintain a good standing with the IRS.

By understanding and fulfilling the annual reporting requirements, you demonstrate your organization's commitment to transparency and accountability. This not only fosters trust among your stakeholders but also ensures that you can continue to enjoy the tax benefits associated with your non-profit status.

In the following chapters, we will delve into other crucial aspects of starting and managing a tax-exempt non-profit organization, such as fundraising, governance, and compliance with federal and state laws.

Compliance with IRS Regulations

When starting a non-profit organization, one of the most crucial steps is ensuring compliance with IRS regulations. The Internal Revenue Service (IRS) is responsible for overseeing tax-exempt organizations and determining their eligibility for tax-exempt status. In this subchapter, we will provide a step-by-step guide on filing for tax-exempt status, helping you navigate the complex process and avoid common pitfalls.

Why is compliance with IRS regulations important? Achieving tax-exempt status not only allows your non-profit organization to receive tax-deductible donations but also provides credibility and legitimacy in the eyes of donors, volunteers, and the community. By adhering to IRS regulations, you demonstrate your commitment to transparency and accountability.

The first step in complying with IRS regulations is to determine the type of tax-exempt status your organization qualifies for. The most common status is 501(c)(3), which covers charitable, educational, religious, and scientific organizations. However, there are other categories, such as 501(c)(4) for social welfare organizations and 501(c)(6) for business leagues. Understanding which category best fits your organization's mission is crucial.

Once you have determined your organization's eligibility, the next step is preparing and filing the necessary documents. This includes completing Form 1023, Application for Recognition of Exemption Under Section 501(c)(3) of the Internal Revenue Code, or Form 1024 for other types of tax-exempt status. These forms require detailed information about your organization's purpose, activities, governance structure, and financial projections.

Completing these forms accurately and thoroughly is vital to avoid delays or potential rejection of your application. It is recommended to seek professional assistance or consult an attorney experienced in non-profit law to ensure all requirements are met.

Additionally, it is essential to establish proper record-keeping and financial management practices to maintain compliance with IRS regulations. This includes maintaining detailed financial records, filing annual information returns (Form 990), and adhering to rules regarding executive compensation.

In conclusion, compliance with IRS regulations is a crucial aspect of starting a tax-exempt non-profit organization. By following the step-by-step guide provided in this subchapter, you will be well-equipped to navigate the process of filing for tax-exempt status. Remember, achieving compliance not only enables your organization to receive tax-deductible donations but also builds trust and credibility within your community.

Maintaining Good Standing with the IRS

Once your non-profit organization has obtained tax-exempt status, it is crucial to maintain good standing with the Internal Revenue Service (IRS). This ensures that your organization continues to enjoy the benefits of tax-exemption and avoids any potential penalties or revocation of its exempt status. In this subchapter, we will discuss the key steps and practices to maintain good standing with the IRS.

1. Compliance with Annual Reporting Requirements: Every tax-exempt organization is required to file an annual information return, either Form 990, 990-EZ, or 990-N. It is important to understand which form your organization needs to file and ensure timely submission. Failure to file or late filing can lead to severe penalties and even loss of tax-exempt status.

2. Maintain Accurate and Complete Records: Proper record-keeping is crucial for any non-profit organization. Maintain detailed records of income, expenses, donations, and any other financial transactions.

These records will not only assist in preparing accurate annual returns but also serve as evidence of your organization's compliance during an IRS audit.

3. Follow Appropriate Financial Management Practices: Ensure your organization adheres to proper financial management practices, including segregating duties, conducting regular internal audits, and implementing strong internal controls. These practices not only promote transparency and accountability but also help safeguard against potential fraud or misuse of funds.

4. Engage in Permissible Activities: Non-profit organizations must ensure that their activities align with their stated mission and comply with IRS regulations. Engaging in excessive unrelated business activities or lobbying beyond permissible limits can jeopardize tax-exempt status. Regularly review your activities and consult legal counsel if uncertain about compliance.

5. Stay Informed and Seek Professional Guidance: Tax laws and regulations are subject to change, and staying informed is essential. Subscribe to IRS newsletters, attend workshops or webinars, and join professional associations to stay updated on any changes that may impact your organization. It is also advisable to work with a knowledgeable tax professional or attorney who specializes in non-profit tax law to ensure ongoing compliance.

Maintaining good standing with the IRS is crucial for any non-profit organization as it allows you to focus on your mission without worrying about tax implications. By complying with annual reporting requirements, maintaining accurate records, following financial management practices, engaging in permissible activities, and staying informed, you can ensure your organization's continued tax-exempt status. Remember, the IRS is there to help and provide guidance, so don't hesitate to reach out if you have any questions or concerns.

Chapter 10: Fundraising Strategies for Non-Profit Organizations

Developing a Fundraising Plan

One of the key elements to successfully starting and sustaining a non-profit organization is having a well-developed fundraising plan. Fundraising is a crucial aspect of any non-profit's operations, as it provides the financial resources necessary to support the organization's mission and programs. In this subchapter, we will guide you through the process of creating an effective fundraising plan for your non-profit.

Step 1: Assess Your Organization's Needs and Goals
Before diving into fundraising strategies, it is important to evaluate your organization's specific needs and goals. Identify the financial resources required to support your programs, projects, and initiatives. Determine the amount of money you need to raise annually and break it down into achievable milestones.

Step 2: Identify Your Target Donors
Knowing your target donors is essential for creating a successful fundraising plan. Research and analyze potential donors who align with your organization's mission and values. Consider individual donors, corporations, foundations, and government agencies that may be interested in supporting your cause.

Step 3: Develop a Mix of Fundraising Strategies
A diverse mix of fundraising strategies will maximize your chances of success. Explore various avenues, such as individual giving, major gifts, corporate sponsorships, grant writing, events, and online

crowdfunding. Each strategy has its own advantages and requires a tailored approach.

Step 4: Set Clear Objectives and Action Steps
To stay on track, set clear objectives and action steps for each fundraising strategy. Define specific fundraising goals, such as the number of donors or the amount of money to be raised. Break these goals down into small, achievable steps, and assign responsibilities to team members.

Step 5: Create a Fundraising Calendar
Developing a fundraising calendar will help you stay organized and ensure that you maximize your fundraising efforts throughout the year. Identify key events, campaigns, and deadlines for grants or sponsorships. Allocate resources and plan your communication and marketing strategies accordingly.

Step 6: Monitor and Evaluate Your Fundraising Efforts
Regularly monitor and evaluate the effectiveness of your fundraising efforts. Track your progress against your goals and adjust your strategies as needed. Analyze the return on investment for each fundraising activity and identify areas for improvement.

Remember, fundraising is an ongoing process that requires dedication, persistence, and creativity. By developing a well-thought-out fundraising plan and executing it with precision, you can secure the financial resources necessary to support your organization's mission and make a meaningful impact in your community.

Identifying Funding Sources

One of the most crucial aspects of starting a non-profit organization is identifying the right funding sources. Without adequate financial support, it can be challenging for a non-profit to sustain its operations and fulfill its mission. In this subchapter, we will explore various funding sources that you can consider for your non-profit organization.

1. Grants: Grants are a popular funding option for non-profit organizations. They are typically provided by foundations, corporations, or government agencies. Grants can be project-specific or general operating support, and they often require a detailed proposal outlining your organization's goals and how the funds will be utilized.

2. Individual Donations: Individual donors play a significant role in supporting non-profit organizations. These donors can be anyone who believes in your cause and wants to contribute financially. To attract individual donors, it is essential to build strong relationships with your supporters, communicate your organization's impact, and create meaningful opportunities for them to get involved.

3. Corporate Sponsorships: Many corporations are willing to support non-profit organizations through sponsorship programs. These sponsorships can provide financial assistance, in-kind donations, or even employee volunteering opportunities. Research corporations that align with your mission and values and reach out to them with a well-crafted proposal that highlights the mutual benefits of a partnership.

4. Fundraising Events: Organizing fundraising events can be an effective way to generate financial support and raise awareness for your non-profit. These events can include galas, charity auctions, walkathons, or online crowdfunding campaigns. Ensure that your

events are well-planned and promoted to attract a wide audience and maximize donations.

5. Membership Fees: If your non-profit offers membership benefits or services, consider charging membership fees. These fees can provide a steady stream of revenue to support your organization's activities. Make sure to offer valuable benefits to your members to encourage ongoing support.

6. Government Contracts: Depending on the nature of your non-profit's work, you may be eligible for government contracts or grants. Research government programs and initiatives that align with your mission and explore opportunities for collaboration or funding.

Remember, a diverse funding strategy is crucial for the long-term sustainability of your non-profit organization. By exploring various funding sources and developing strong relationships with donors, corporations, and government agencies, you can ensure a stable financial foundation for your non-profit's important work.

In the upcoming chapters, we will delve deeper into each funding source, providing practical tips on how to approach and secure funding from each avenue. Understanding the intricacies of each funding source and tailoring your approach accordingly will significantly increase your chances of securing the necessary resources to fulfill your non-profit's mission.

Implementing Fundraising Campaigns

One of the key pillars of running a successful non-profit organization is the ability to raise funds effectively. Fundraising campaigns play a crucial role in generating financial resources for your cause and ensuring the sustainability of your organization. In this subchapter, we will explore the essential steps and strategies involved in implementing fundraising campaigns for your tax-exempt non-profit.

1. Set Clear Goals: Before launching a fundraising campaign, it is vital to define your objectives. Determine the specific amount of money you need to raise and the purpose for which the funds will be utilized. Clear goals will not only help you stay focused but also provide a sense of direction to your potential donors.

2. Identify Target Donors: Understanding your target audience is essential for a successful fundraising campaign. Identify potential donors who align with your organization's mission and values. This can include individuals, corporations, foundations, or even government grants. Tailor your fundraising approach based on their preferences and interests.

3. Craft a Compelling Message: Develop a compelling case statement that clearly communicates the importance of your cause. Your message should evoke emotions and inspire potential donors to take action. Highlight the impact their contribution can make and how it aligns with their own values and aspirations.

4. Diversify Fundraising Methods: To maximize your chances of success, diversify your fundraising methods. Consider a mix of traditional and digital strategies such as direct mail, events, online crowdfunding, peer-to-peer fundraising, and corporate sponsorships. Each approach has its own advantages and can help you reach different segments of your target audience.

5. Create a Fundraising Plan: Develop a comprehensive fundraising plan that outlines your strategies, tactics, and timelines. This plan will

act as a roadmap for your fundraising efforts and ensure that you stay on track. It should include a budget, marketing strategies, volunteer engagement, and donor stewardship plans.

6. Build Strong Relationships: Cultivating strong relationships with your donors is essential for long-term sustainability. Provide regular updates on your organization's progress, express gratitude for their contributions, and engage them in your initiatives. Personalized communication and recognition can go a long way in building trust and loyalty.

7. Evaluate and Improve: Continuously evaluate the effectiveness of your fundraising campaigns and make necessary improvements. Monitor key performance indicators such as funds raised, donor retention rates, and cost per dollar raised. Use this data to refine your strategies and enhance future campaigns.

Remember, fundraising is an ongoing process, and building a strong support base takes time. Stay committed, adapt to changing trends, and always prioritize transparency and accountability. By implementing effective fundraising campaigns, you can provide a solid financial foundation for your non-profit organization and make a lasting impact in your community.

Chapter 11: Financial Management for Non-Profit Organizations

Budgeting and Financial Planning

When it comes to starting a non-profit organization, one of the most crucial aspects to consider is budgeting and financial planning. Creating a solid financial foundation is essential for the long-term success and sustainability of any non-profit. In this subchapter, we will guide you through the process of budgeting and financial planning, providing you with the necessary tools and knowledge to make informed decisions.

Budgeting is the process of estimating income and expenses over a specified period. It serves as a roadmap for your organization's financial activities, ensuring that resources are allocated efficiently and effectively. To begin the budgeting process, you must first identify your sources of income. This may include donations, grants, membership fees, or revenue from fundraising events. By understanding your income streams, you can develop a realistic budget that aligns with your organization's goals and objectives.

Once you have identified your sources of income, it is important to determine your expenses. This includes both fixed costs, such as rent and utilities, as well as variable costs, such as program expenses and marketing. It is crucial to allocate resources wisely, ensuring that your expenses do not exceed your income. Creating a detailed budget that accounts for every expense will help you make informed financial decisions and avoid any surprises down the road.

In addition to budgeting, financial planning is equally important for the success of your non-profit organization. Financial planning involves setting financial goals, developing strategies to achieve them, and monitoring your progress. By setting clear objectives, you can create a roadmap for your organization's financial growth and sustainability.

Furthermore, financial planning includes creating reserves or emergency funds to address unexpected expenses or economic downturns. Establishing a reserve fund is a prudent approach, as it provides a safety net for your organization during challenging times.

To ensure accurate and transparent financial reporting, it is essential to implement proper accounting and bookkeeping practices. Maintaining accurate records will not only help you track your organization's financial health but also ensure compliance with legal and regulatory requirements.

In conclusion, budgeting and financial planning are critical components of starting and managing a non-profit organization. By carefully estimating income and expenses, setting financial goals, and implementing sound accounting practices, you can create a strong financial foundation for your organization's success. Remember, financial stability is not only essential for your organization's day-to-day operations but also for attracting donors and stakeholders who share your vision.

Accounting and Bookkeeping Practices

Accurate and transparent financial management is crucial for the success and credibility of any non-profit organization. In this subchapter, we will delve into the essential accounting and bookkeeping practices that every aspiring non-profit founder should be familiar with. By implementing these practices, you can ensure that your organization operates smoothly, meets legal obligations, and maintains the trust of donors and stakeholders.

1. Establishing a Chart of Accounts: A chart of accounts is the foundation of your organization's financial system. It categorizes all income, expenses, assets, and liabilities, enabling you to track and manage your financial transactions effectively. We will guide you through the process of setting up a chart of accounts tailored to your non-profit's specific needs.

2. Tracking Donations and Grants: Non-profit organizations heavily rely on donations and grants, which must be accurately recorded and tracked. We will discuss best practices for documenting contributions, including cash, in-kind donations, and grants. Additionally, we will explore the importance of maintaining detailed donor records to foster strong relationships and facilitate future fundraising efforts.

3. Budgeting and Financial Planning: Developing a comprehensive budget is crucial for non-profits to allocate resources effectively and achieve their mission. We will provide a step-by-step guide on creating a budget that reflects your organization's goals and priorities. Furthermore, we will explore techniques for financial forecasting and monitoring performance to ensure that your non-profit remains financially sustainable.

4. Compliance with Reporting Requirements: Non-profit organizations are subject to various reporting obligations to maintain tax-exempt status and transparency. We will walk you through the necessary financial statements, such as the statement of activities, statement of financial position, and statement of cash flows. Understanding these reports will help you fulfill legal requirements and provide stakeholders with clear insights into your organization's financial health.

5. Internal Controls and Auditing: Implementing strong internal controls is essential to prevent fraud, errors, and mismanagement of funds. We will discuss the importance of segregation of duties, regular financial reviews, and independent auditing. By establishing these practices, you can safeguard your non-profit's assets and ensure financial accountability.

6. Utilizing Accounting Software: Adopting modern accounting software can streamline your organization's financial processes, enhance accuracy, and save time. We will introduce you to popular accounting software options and guide you through selecting the most suitable one for your non-profit.

Whether you have previous accounting knowledge or not, this subchapter will equip you with the fundamental accounting and bookkeeping practices necessary to start and effectively manage your tax-exempt non-profit organization. By adhering to these practices, you will build a solid financial foundation and increase the likelihood of achieving your organization's mission.

Grant Management and Reporting

One of the key aspects of successfully running a tax-exempt non-profit organization is efficient grant management and reporting. Grants play a vital role in funding the initiatives and programs of non-profits, allowing them to make a significant impact on the communities they serve. This subchapter will provide a step-by-step guide on grant management and reporting, ensuring that your non-profit organization can effectively secure and utilize grant funds.

The first step in grant management is to identify potential grant opportunities that align with your non-profit's mission and objectives. This involves conducting thorough research and staying updated on available grants from government agencies, foundations, corporations, and other funding sources. Understanding the eligibility criteria, application process, and deadlines for each grant will help you make informed decisions about which grants to pursue.

Once you have identified a grant opportunity, it is crucial to carefully review the grant guidelines and requirements. This includes understanding the budgetary restrictions, reporting obligations, and any specific deliverables or outcomes expected by the grantor. By thoroughly understanding these requirements, you can develop a realistic and comprehensive plan for utilizing the grant funds effectively.

Proper record-keeping is essential for successful grant management. Establishing a system to track all expenses, activities, and outcomes related to the grant will help ensure compliance with reporting requirements. This includes maintaining accurate financial records, receipts, and documentation of program activities and progress. Regularly reviewing and reconciling financial records will allow you to identify any discrepancies and address them promptly.

Reporting is a critical aspect of grant management. Most grant agreements require periodic reports to track the progress and impact of the funded programs. These reports may include financial statements, narrative descriptions of activities, and quantitative data on outcomes achieved. Timely and accurate reporting demonstrates accountability and transparency, which can enhance your organization's reputation and increase the likelihood of future grant funding.

In conclusion, grant management and reporting are essential for the success of any tax-exempt non-profit organization. By following a step-by-step guide, you can effectively identify, secure, and utilize grant funds to advance your mission. Implementing a robust record-keeping system and adhering to reporting requirements will ensure compliance and build trust with grantors. With proper grant management and reporting, your non-profit can make a lasting impact on the communities you serve.

Chapter 12: Marketing and Promoting Your Non-Profit

Developing a Marketing Strategy

In today's competitive world, non-profit organizations need to have a well-thought-out marketing strategy to effectively promote their mission, attract donors, and engage with their target audience. A strong marketing strategy helps non-profit organizations build awareness, generate support, and ultimately achieve their goals. This subchapter will guide you through the process of developing an effective marketing strategy for your non-profit organization.

Step 1: Understand Your Target Audience
To develop a successful marketing strategy, it is crucial to understand your target audience. Identify who your non-profit organization aims to serve and the individuals or groups who are most likely to support your cause. Conduct market research, surveys, and focus groups to gain insights into their needs, preferences, and motivations.

Step 2: Define Your Unique Selling Proposition (USP)
Your non-profit organization needs to have a compelling USP that differentiates it from similar organizations. Determine what sets you apart and highlight the unique value you offer to your audience. This could be your innovative approach, the impact you have made, or the specific problem you are addressing.

Step 3: Set Clear Goals and Objectives
Your marketing strategy should align with your organization's overall goals and objectives. Establish specific, measurable, achievable, relevant, and time-bound (SMART) goals for your marketing efforts.

Whether you aim to increase donations, raise awareness, or recruit volunteers, having clear objectives will guide your marketing activities.

Step 4: Choose the Right Marketing Channels
Identify the most effective marketing channels to reach your target audience. This could include social media platforms, email marketing, content creation, traditional media, events, or partnerships with other organizations. Select channels that are popular among your target audience and align with your organization's resources and capabilities.

Step 5: Create Compelling Content
Develop engaging and persuasive content that communicates your non-profit's mission, impact, and goals. Use storytelling techniques to emotionally connect with your audience and inspire them to take action. Leverage visuals, videos, and testimonials to effectively convey your message.

Step 6: Implement and Measure Your Strategy
Once you have developed your marketing strategy, implement it across the chosen channels. Monitor and measure the effectiveness of your marketing efforts regularly. Track key performance indicators (KPIs) such as website traffic, social media engagement, donor conversions, and volunteer sign-ups. Analyze the data to identify areas for improvement and make necessary adjustments to optimize your strategy.

By developing a comprehensive marketing strategy, your non-profit organization can effectively promote its mission, attract support, and achieve its goals. Remember that marketing is an ongoing process, and it is important to continuously evaluate and adapt your strategy to stay relevant and impactful in an ever-evolving landscape.

Creating a Strong Brand Identity

In the competitive landscape of the non-profit sector, developing a strong brand identity is essential for the success and sustainability of your organization. A strong brand identity not only helps you stand out from the crowd but also allows you to effectively communicate your mission and values to your target audience. This subchapter will guide you through the process of creating a compelling brand identity for your tax-exempt non-profit organization.

1. Defining Your Mission and Values:
Before diving into the brand identity creation process, it is crucial to have a clear understanding of your organization's mission and values. Your mission statement should be concise yet powerful, conveying the core purpose of your non-profit. Similarly, defining your organization's values will help shape your brand identity and guide decision-making processes.

2. Conducting Market Research:
To create a strong brand identity, you must understand your target audience and their needs. Conduct market research to identify the demographics, psychographics, and preferences of your potential supporters and donors. This information will help you tailor your brand identity to effectively engage and resonate with your audience.

3. Developing a Compelling Visual Identity:
Your visual identity plays a significant role in shaping your brand. Design a logo that reflects your non-profit's mission and values while being visually appealing and memorable. Ensure consistency in the use of colors, fonts, and imagery across all your communication channels, including your website, social media profiles, and marketing materials.

4. Crafting a Consistent Brand Voice:
Your brand voice is the personality and tone you use to communicate with your audience. Identify the voice that best represents your organization and aligns with your mission and values. Whether it is formal, friendly, or authoritative, consistency in your brand voice will help build trust and recognition among your stakeholders.

5. Creating a Compelling Brand Message:
Craft a compelling brand message that encapsulates your mission, values, and impact. This message should clearly communicate the unique value your non-profit brings to the table, inspiring people to support your cause and contribute to your organization's success.

6. Engaging with Your Audience:
Building a strong brand identity requires active engagement with your audience. Leverage social media platforms, email newsletters, and community events to connect with your supporters and donors. Regularly communicate your organization's accomplishments, impact stories, and upcoming initiatives to keep your audience engaged and connected to your cause.

Remember, creating a strong brand identity is an ongoing process. Continuously monitor and evaluate your brand's performance and adapt it as needed to keep up with changing trends and audience preferences. By investing time and effort into building a compelling brand identity, you will position your tax-exempt non-profit organization for long-term success and impact in your community.

Utilizing Digital Marketing and Social Media

In today's digital age, the power of digital marketing and social media cannot be underestimated, especially when it comes to starting a tax-exempt non-profit organization. This subchapter will provide you with a comprehensive guide on how to effectively utilize digital marketing and social media to promote your non-profit, attract donors, and engage with your target audience.

1. Building an Online Presence:
Creating a professional and engaging website is essential for any non-profit organization. Your website should reflect your mission, values, and goals. It should also include clear calls to action and ways for visitors to donate or get involved. Additionally, optimize your website for search engines to ensure that it ranks high in search results.

2. Social Media Strategy:
Social media platforms such as Facebook, Instagram, Twitter, and LinkedIn offer incredible opportunities to reach a wide audience and amplify your message. Develop a social media strategy that aligns with your non-profit's goals and target audience. Regularly post engaging content, share success stories, promote events, and encourage followers to share your posts. Use hashtags relevant to your cause to increase visibility.

3. Content Marketing:
Content is king! Develop a content marketing strategy to establish yourself as an authoritative voice in your niche. Create informative articles, blog posts, videos, and infographics that provide value to your target audience. Share this content on your website and social media platforms to attract and engage potential donors and volunteers.

4. Email Marketing:
Email marketing remains an effective tool for engaging with your audience. Build an email list by offering valuable resources or incentives to sign up. Regularly send out newsletters, impact stories, event invitations, and fundraising appeals to keep your supporters informed and engaged.

5. Online Fundraising:
Digital platforms offer numerous ways to raise funds online. Set up a secure and user-friendly online donation system on your website. Explore crowdfunding platforms like GoFundMe or Kickstarter to reach a wider audience. Leverage social media to launch fundraising campaigns and encourage your followers to share and donate.

6. Analytics and Tracking:
Utilize digital analytics tools such as Google Analytics to track and measure the success of your digital marketing efforts. Monitor website traffic, social media engagement, email open rates, and donation conversion rates. Use these insights to refine your strategies and increase your impact.

By effectively utilizing digital marketing and social media, you can significantly enhance your non-profit organization's visibility, engagement, and fundraising efforts. Embrace the power of the digital world to connect with your target audience, achieve your mission, and make a lasting impact in your community.

Chapter 13: Building Relationships and Collaborations

Networking with Other Non-Profit Organizations

Building a strong network with other non-profit organizations is essential for the success and growth of your own non-profit. Collaborating and partnering with like-minded organizations can help you amplify your impact, gain access to resources, and foster meaningful relationships within the sector.

1. Why Network with Other Non-Profits?
Networking with other non-profits provides numerous benefits. Firstly, it allows you to tap into a vast pool of knowledge and experience. By connecting with organizations that have similar missions or goals, you can learn from their successes and challenges, gaining valuable insights that can inform your own strategies. Additionally, networking helps you stay up to date with industry trends and best practices, ensuring your non-profit remains relevant in a fast-paced and ever-evolving sector.

2. Identify Potential Partners
Start by identifying potential non-profit partners that align with your mission. Research organizations that share similar values, work in related areas, or have complementary programs. Attend conferences, workshops, and community events to meet representatives from these organizations and initiate conversations. Utilize online platforms and directories specific to non-profits to find potential partners in your area or beyond.

3. Building Relationships
Networking is all about building relationships, so take the time to establish genuine connections with other non-profits. Attend networking events, join industry associations or working groups, and actively engage in conversations. Share your expertise and offer assistance when appropriate, as this will help you gain credibility and trust within the non-profit community. Building strong relationships will open doors to collaborations, joint projects, and mutual support.

4. Collaborative Opportunities
Look for opportunities to collaborate with other non-profits on projects or initiatives that align with your mission. By pooling your resources, you can achieve greater impact and reach a wider audience. Collaborative efforts can include joint fundraising campaigns, shared programs or events, or even partnering on advocacy or policy initiatives. Remember, collaboration is a two-way street, so be open to supporting other non-profits as well.

5. Resource Sharing
Networking with other non-profits also provides access to valuable resources. These can range from sharing best practices, templates, and tools to accessing training or capacity-building opportunities. By collaborating with organizations that have complementary strengths, you can tap into their expertise and resources, enhancing your own organization's capacity to fulfill its mission.

In conclusion, networking with other non-profit organizations is a crucial step in starting and growing a tax-exempt non-profit. By building relationships, seeking collaborative opportunities, and sharing resources, you can amplify your impact and create a stronger non-profit sector overall. Remember, the key to successful networking lies in initiating and nurturing meaningful connections, so be proactive in reaching out and engaging with other non-profits in your community and beyond.

Establishing Partnerships with Businesses and Foundations

In the world of non-profit organizations, partnerships with businesses and foundations can be the key to success. These partnerships can offer a wide range of benefits, including financial support, resources, expertise, and increased visibility. In this subchapter, we will explore how to effectively establish and nurture partnerships with businesses and foundations, empowering you with the tools you need to take your non-profit organization to the next level.

1. Identifying potential partners: The first step in establishing partnerships is to identify businesses and foundations that align with your mission and values. Look for organizations that have a history of supporting causes similar to yours, as well as those that may have a personal connection to your cause.

2. Building relationships: Once you have identified potential partners, it is crucial to build genuine relationships with them. Attend networking events, reach out to key individuals, and find ways to connect on a personal level. Show your passion for your cause and be prepared to articulate how a partnership would be mutually beneficial.

3. Crafting win-win partnerships: Successful partnerships are built on mutual benefit. Clearly define what your organization can offer in return for support, whether it be access to your network, promotional opportunities, or volunteer opportunities for their employees. Make sure to emphasize the value your organization brings to the table.

4. Developing a partnership proposal: When approaching potential partners, it is essential to have a well-crafted partnership proposal. This proposal should outline your organization's mission, goals, and the specific ways in which you envision partnering with the business or foundation. Be clear about what you are seeking and how it aligns with their interests.

5. Nurturing and maintaining partnerships: Once a partnership is established, it is crucial to nurture and maintain it. Keep communication lines open, provide regular updates on your organization's progress, and show appreciation for their support. Regularly evaluate the partnership's effectiveness and make adjustments as needed to ensure both parties are benefiting.

6. Leveraging partnerships for growth: As your non-profit organization grows, your partnerships with businesses and foundations can play a pivotal role in expanding your impact. Look for opportunities to collaborate on larger initiatives, seek their guidance on strategic planning, and leverage their expertise and resources to achieve your goals.

Establishing partnerships with businesses and foundations is an invaluable strategy for starting and growing a tax-exempt non-profit organization. By following these steps and fostering meaningful relationships, you can create partnerships that not only provide financial support but also contribute to your organization's long-term success. Remember, effective partnerships are built on mutual trust, shared values, and a commitment to making a difference in the world.

Engaging with the Local Community

Building strong relationships with the local community is a vital aspect of starting and running a tax-exempt non-profit organization. Engaging with the community not only helps you establish a positive reputation but also enables you to gain support and resources that are essential for the success of your organization.

One of the first steps in engaging with the local community is to conduct thorough research to identify the needs and interests of the community members. By understanding their concerns, you can tailor your non-profit's mission and programs to address those specific issues. This will not only make your organization more relevant but also increase its chances of making a meaningful impact.

Once you have identified the community's needs, it is time to establish partnerships and collaborations. Reach out to local businesses, schools, churches, and other non-profit organizations to explore potential collaborations. These partnerships can help you access additional resources, such as funding, volunteers, and space for events or programs. Collaborating with established organizations also lends credibility to your non-profit, making it easier to gain the trust of the community.

Engaging with the community also involves active participation in community events and initiatives. Attend local meetings, festivals, and fundraisers to network with community members and raise awareness about your organization's mission. This will help you connect with potential donors, volunteers, and supporters who may share your passion for the cause.

An effective way to engage with the local community is to provide educational opportunities. Organize workshops, seminars, or training sessions that address the community's concerns or provide valuable skills. By offering these services, you position your non-profit as a valuable resource and build trust within the community.

Lastly, don't forget the power of social media and online platforms in engaging with the local community. Establish a strong online presence by creating a website and regularly updating your social media accounts. Use these platforms to share success stories, upcoming events, and volunteer opportunities to keep the community informed and engaged.

In conclusion, engaging with the local community is a crucial step in starting and running a tax-exempt non-profit organization. By understanding the community's needs, establishing partnerships, participating in community events, providing education, and utilizing online platforms, you can build strong relationships, gain support, and make a lasting impact on the community you serve.

Chapter 14: Evaluating and Scaling Your Non-Profit

Monitoring and Evaluating Program Impact

Once your non-profit organization is up and running, it is crucial to monitor and evaluate the impact of your programs. This step is essential to ensure that your organization is effectively fulfilling its mission and making a positive difference in the community it serves. In this subchapter, we will explore the importance of monitoring and evaluating program impact and provide you with a step-by-step guide to effectively measure and assess your organization's success.

Monitoring and evaluating program impact allows you to gather evidence and data to determine whether your programs are achieving their intended outcomes. It helps you identify areas of strength and areas that need improvement, enabling you to make informed decisions and adjustments for the benefit of your organization and the community it serves.

To begin monitoring and evaluating your program impact, you must start by defining clear goals and objectives for each program. These goals should be specific, measurable, achievable, relevant, and time-bound (SMART). By setting SMART goals, you will have a clear framework for assessing whether your programs are achieving their intended outcomes.

Once you have established your goals, you can develop appropriate monitoring and evaluation mechanisms. This may include collecting data through surveys, interviews, focus groups, or reviewing existing records and reports. It is important to collect both qualitative and quantitative data to gain a comprehensive understanding of your program's impact.

Regularly reviewing and analyzing the data you collect is crucial. This will allow you to identify trends, patterns, and areas of success or improvement. It is also important to involve stakeholders, such as program participants, volunteers, and staff, in the evaluation process. Their input can provide valuable insights and perspectives.

Based on your findings, you can make informed decisions and adjustments to your programs. This may involve reallocating resources, modifying program activities, or implementing new strategies to enhance impact. By continuously monitoring and evaluating your program impact, you can ensure that your organization remains focused on its mission and adapts to the evolving needs of the community it serves.

In conclusion, monitoring and evaluating program impact is a vital aspect of running a successful non-profit organization. It allows you to assess your organization's effectiveness, make informed decisions, and continually improve your programs. By following the step-by-step guide provided in this subchapter, you will be equipped with the necessary tools and knowledge to effectively measure and evaluate your non-profit organization's impact.

Scaling Up Your Non-Profit's Operations

When starting a non-profit organization, it is essential to have a clear vision and mission. However, as your organization grows and gains traction, it becomes necessary to scale up your operations to be able to make a more significant impact on your cause. Scaling up your non-profit's operations requires careful planning and strategic thinking. In this subchapter, we will guide you through the process of scaling up your non-profit organization effectively.

1. Assess your current operations: Before scaling up, it is crucial to evaluate your organization's current operations. Identify any bottlenecks or areas that need improvement. This assessment will help you understand where to focus your efforts when scaling up.

2. Set clear goals: Define specific and measurable goals for your organization's growth. These goals will act as a roadmap for scaling up and provide direction for your team. Make sure your goals align with your mission and vision.

3. Build a strong team: Scaling up requires a dedicated and passionate team. Assess your current team's skills and determine if any additional talent is required. Recruit individuals who are aligned with your organization's values and can contribute to its growth.

4. Establish strategic partnerships: Collaborating with like-minded organizations and individuals can significantly enhance your non-profit's impact. Identify potential partners who can support your mission and explore mutually beneficial partnerships.

5. Secure funding: Scaling up often requires additional financial resources. Develop a comprehensive fundraising strategy to secure funding for your organization's expansion. This may involve applying for grants, organizing fundraising events, or soliciting donations from corporate sponsors and individual donors.

6. Leverage technology: Technology can streamline your operations and enable you to reach a wider audience. Invest in appropriate

software and tools that can automate administrative tasks, enhance communication, and improve efficiency.

7. Develop effective systems and processes: As you scale up, it is crucial to establish efficient systems and processes to handle increased workload and maintain quality standards. This includes setting up robust financial management, volunteer management, and program evaluation systems.

8. Monitor and evaluate: Regularly monitor and evaluate your organization's progress towards its goals. This will help you identify any shortcomings and make necessary adjustments to ensure successful scaling up.

Scaling up your non-profit organization's operations can be a challenging but rewarding endeavor. By following these steps and continuously learning and adapting, you can effectively expand your organization's reach and make a more significant impact on your cause.

Remember, scaling up is a gradual process that requires patience and perseverance. Stay committed to your mission, and with careful planning and strategic execution, you can take your non-profit to new heights.

Ensuring Long-Term Sustainability

One of the key factors in the success of any non-profit organization is its long-term sustainability. Without a solid foundation and a strategic plan for the future, even the most well-intentioned initiatives can falter and fail. In this subchapter, we will explore the crucial steps you need to take to ensure the long-term sustainability of your non-profit organization.

1. Mission and Vision: The first step towards long-term sustainability is to clearly define your organization's mission and vision. These guiding principles will serve as the compass for your organization's activities and will help you stay focused on your goals. Regularly revisit and evaluate your mission and vision to ensure they remain relevant and aligned with your organization's purpose.

2. Strategic Planning: Developing a comprehensive strategic plan is essential to the long-term success of your non-profit. This plan should outline your organization's goals, objectives, and strategies for achieving them. It should also include a timeline and milestones for measuring progress. Regularly review and update your strategic plan to adapt to changing circumstances and to ensure you are on track to achieve your goals.

3. Fundraising and Financial Management: Non-profit organizations heavily rely on fundraising to sustain their operations. Develop a diverse fundraising strategy that includes individual donations, grants, corporate sponsorships, and fundraising events. Additionally, establish sound financial management practices to ensure transparency and accountability. Regularly assess your financial health and make adjustments as needed.

4. Building Relationships: Cultivating strong relationships with donors, volunteers, and community partners is crucial for the long-term sustainability of your organization. Regularly communicate with your stakeholders, express gratitude, and demonstrate the impact of their support. Engage with your community through outreach events and partnerships to expand your network and build a strong support base.

5. Board Development: Your organization's board of directors plays a vital role in its long-term success. Ensure you have a diverse and

engaged board that is committed to your mission. Regularly assess your board's effectiveness and provide ongoing training and development opportunities to enhance their skills and knowledge.

6. Evaluation and Continuous Improvement: Regularly evaluate your organization's programs and activities to measure their effectiveness and impact. Use this feedback to make informed decisions and continuously improve your operations. Embrace a culture of learning and adaptability to stay relevant and responsive to the needs of your beneficiaries.

By following these steps and implementing a strategic approach, you can ensure the long-term sustainability of your non-profit organization. Remember, building a successful non-profit takes time, effort, and dedication, but the impact you can make on your community and the world is well worth it.

Chapter 15: Conclusion and Next Steps

Celebrating Achievements

Starting a non-profit organization is a monumental task that requires dedication, passion, and perseverance. It takes countless hours of hard work, strategic planning, and financial management to turn an idea into a fully functioning tax-exempt entity. Along this journey, it is important to acknowledge and celebrate the achievements that come along the way. This subchapter will explore the significance of celebrating milestones and accomplishments in the process of starting a non-profit organization.

When embarking on the path of creating a tax-exempt non-profit, it is easy to become overwhelmed by the challenges and obstacles that may arise. However, it is crucial to recognize and celebrate the achievements, no matter how small they may seem. Celebrating serves as a motivator, boosting morale and encouraging continued dedication to the cause.

One of the initial achievements to celebrate is the completion of the strategic plan. Developing a clear vision, mission, and goals for your non-profit organization is a significant milestone. It sets the foundation for your organization's future and demonstrates your commitment to making a difference in your chosen niche. Take the time to acknowledge this accomplishment, either individually or with your team, and use it as a reminder of the impact you are striving to make.

Another achievement worth celebrating is the successful filing for tax-exempt status. This step is crucial for any non-profit organization, as it provides legal recognition and tax benefits. Navigating the complex process of filing for tax-exemption can be daunting, but once completed, it is cause for celebration. Share this achievement with your supporters, volunteers, and donors, as it showcases the legitimacy and credibility of your organization.

Fundraising milestones should also be recognized and celebrated. Raising funds is essential for the sustainability of any non-profit organization. Whether it's reaching a certain donation target, securing a grant, or organizing a successful fundraising event, these achievements highlight the support and belief in your cause. Celebrate these milestones with your team and supporters to show gratitude and acknowledge their contributions to your organization's growth.

In conclusion, celebrating achievements throughout the process of starting a non-profit organization is essential for motivation and morale. Whether it's the completion of a strategic plan, the successful filing for tax-exempt status, or reaching fundraising milestones, each accomplishment brings you one step closer to making a difference in your chosen niche. By taking the time to celebrate these achievements, you not only acknowledge the hard work and dedication invested but also inspire continued efforts towards achieving your organization's goals.

Continuing Growth and Improvement

Once you have successfully obtained tax-exempt status for your non-profit organization, the journey is far from over. In fact, it is just the beginning of an exciting and fulfilling adventure. In this subchapter, we will explore the various ways in which you can ensure the continuing growth and improvement of your non-profit organization.

One of the key factors in the success of any non-profit organization is having a clear vision and mission. As times change and society evolves, it is essential to periodically review and refine your organization's purpose to ensure its relevance and effectiveness. Engage with your team and stakeholders to identify any necessary adjustments to your mission statement and long-term goals, keeping in mind the needs of the community you serve.

Fundraising is an ongoing process that requires dedication and creativity. Developing a comprehensive fundraising strategy will help you secure the financial resources necessary to support your programs and initiatives. Explore various avenues such as grants, sponsorships, events, and individual donations to diversify your funding sources. Regularly assess the effectiveness of your fundraising efforts and make necessary adjustments to ensure maximum impact.

Building strong relationships with your supporters and donors is crucial for the sustainability of your organization. Maintain open lines of communication and express gratitude for their contributions, whether big or small. Keep them informed about the impact their support has had on your organization's mission and provide regular updates on your projects and accomplishments. Cultivating a sense of community and involvement will create a loyal network of supporters who will continue to champion your cause.

Collaboration with other non-profit organizations and community partners can significantly enhance your organization's impact. Identify like-minded organizations with complementary missions and explore opportunities for joint projects and initiatives. By pooling resources and expertise, you can achieve greater efficiency and effectiveness in addressing the needs of your community.

Continuous evaluation and improvement are vital aspects of any successful non-profit organization. Regularly assess your programs, projects, and operations to identify areas for improvement. Solicit feedback from your beneficiaries, volunteers, and staff to gain insights into what is working well and what can be enhanced. Embrace a culture of learning and adaptability, always striving for excellence in your endeavors.

In conclusion, obtaining tax-exempt status is just the first step in the journey of building a successful non-profit organization. By continuously evaluating, refining, and improving your vision, fundraising efforts, relationships, partnerships, and operations, you can ensure the ongoing growth and impact of your non-profit. Embrace the challenges and opportunities that come your way, and remember that your organization has the power to make a real difference in the lives of those you serve.

Resources and Further Assistance

Starting a tax-exempt non-profit organization can be a complex and daunting process. However, with the right resources and assistance, you can navigate through the steps effectively and efficiently. This subchapter aims to provide you with a comprehensive list of useful resources and support that will help you in your journey from idea to exemption.

1. Government Websites: The Internal Revenue Service (IRS) website is a vital resource for anyone looking to start a tax-exempt non-profit organization. The IRS provides detailed information on the application process, forms, guidelines, and regulations. Additionally, many state governments have their own websites with relevant information and forms specific to your location.

2. Non-Profit Organizations: There are numerous non-profit organizations that offer guidance and support to those starting their own tax-exempt organizations. These organizations often provide free or low-cost workshops, webinars, and training programs on topics ranging from legal compliance to fundraising strategies. The National Council of Nonprofits, Nonprofit Tech for Good, and Nonprofit Quarterly are just a few examples of organizations that can be valuable resources.

3. Books and Guides: There are several comprehensive books and guides available that provide step-by-step instructions on starting a tax-exempt non-profit organization. "From Idea to Exemption: A Comprehensive Guide for Starting a Tax-Exempt Non-Profit" is an excellent resource that covers all the necessary aspects of the process. Additionally, books like "Starting and Managing a Nonprofit Organization: A Legal Guide" by Bruce R. Hopkins and "Non-Profit Kit For Dummies" by Stan Hutton and Frances Phillips can provide valuable insights and practical advice.

4. Online Communities and Forums: Engaging with online communities and forums can be a great way to connect with like-minded individuals and seek advice from those who have already gone through the process. Platforms like Reddit, LinkedIn groups, and Facebook groups dedicated to non-profit organizations can provide a wealth of knowledge and support.

5. Professional Assistance: If you feel overwhelmed or unsure about certain aspects of the process, seeking professional assistance is highly recommended. Lawyers specializing in non-profit law and accountants experienced in working with tax-exempt organizations can provide invaluable guidance and ensure compliance with all legal and financial requirements.

Remember, starting a tax-exempt non-profit organization is a significant undertaking, but with the right resources and assistance, you can navigate the process successfully. Utilize the above-mentioned resources to educate yourself, seek guidance, and ensure that you are taking the necessary steps to achieve tax-exempt status for your non-profit organization.

www.ingramcontent.com/pod-product-compliance
Lightning Source LLC
Chambersburg PA
CBHW062352290526
45794CB00005B/2194